21

PRINCIPLES OF HOW TO BE A SUCCESSFUL CAREER STRIPPER

"A New Booty on Duty Guide"

By: Sexy Red Magic City

Certified Triple OG; 21 years in the game

© 2022 The Sexy Red Brand LLC. All rights reserved. No portion of this book may be reproduced in any form without permission from the publisher, except as permitted by U.S. copyright law. For permissions contact: info@thesexyredbrand.com

DEDICATION

This e-book is intended for all the new faces new to the strip club game, to any of my New Booties on Duty whose advice is solicited! After 21 years of dancing, this is the advice I would give, in 21 Principles, if/when asked. Now, this is just my opinion, the way I did things, and even some things I could have done better. And I will tell you this, these principles aren't going to help you finesse customers, or to learn how to turn a customer into a loyal trick, beat a b*tches ass if she trys you, or anything like that. This e-book is not about chasing the bag, but letting it come to you. It is about learning to love, respect, motivate and encourage your fellow sister stripper, within reason. (*don't get taken advantage of now!) And to help show a way to tread lightly in alligator invested waters, while receiving as few bruises as possible. Not to say stripping is all bad, because God knows I've had the time of my life on plenty of occasion! Making lots of money, partying with friends, homies, the rich and the famous…it was SUPER lit! Read "48 Laws of Power" by Robert Greene, if you haven't already. You've got to be purposeful and intentional in this world and move assertively no matter what the conditions. Or not, it's your choice, your experience. Hopefully, after reading this, you feel like you've walked away with some useful gems from it.

Contents

PRINCIPLE 1: Identify what talent you have! (Practice it & Perfect it!) 6
PRINCIPLE 2: Walk that Walk! Be Assertive! 8
PRINCIPLE 3: Master Stage Presence 9
PRINCIPLE 4: Appearance is EVERYTHING!!! 10
PRINCIPLE 5: Attitude is EVERYTHING! 16
PRINCIPLE 6: Teamwork Makes the Dream Work! 17
PRINCIPLE 7: Secure Your Bag & your things! Literally! 19
PRINCIPLE 8: Promote Your Brand; Social Media, word-of-mouth 20
PRINCIPLE 9: Use the club to Network 22
PRINCIPLE 10: Always, Always, Be Aware of your surroundings! 23
PRINCIPLE 11: Don't take everything to heart, or personal. 24
PRINCIPLE 12: Don't bring a gun to a knife fight choose your battles 25
PRINCIPLE 13: Do things you like; things that make YOU feel good. .. 26
PRINCIPLE 14: Cater to your customers; pay special attention to them AND their lady guests. 27
PRINCIPLE 15: Exclusivity: Don't allow yourself to be SMUTTED out . 28
PRINCIPLE 16: Body Enhancements; Do what makes YOU happy. 30
PRINCIPLE 17: Do NOT make promises you cannot keep! 31
PRINCIPLE 18: Know your Worth! 32
PRINCIPLE 19: Don't become a lush! 34
PRINCIPLE 20: Sometimes You Gotta Take the Good with the Bad. ... 36
PRINCIPLE 21: Have an Exit Plan 38
BONUS PRINCIPLE: Visualize and Materialize. 40
ABOUT THE AUTHOR 41

PRINCIPLE 1:

Identify what talent you have! (Practice it & Perfect it!)

I remember many times, I would be invited to dance with a group of girls and sometimes how one would lean over and jokingly whisper, "I can't do that. Don't go so hard girl, you're going to make me look bad"! I'd always reply, "Girl, don't worry about me! Do what you do and I'm gonna do what I do! This would be a very boring world if we all did the same thing!" A lot of us have the terrible tendency to compare ourselves to one another. Downplaying ourselves because we feel that our own gifts don't measure up. I say, bump that! Figure out what you're good at and PERFECT the heck out of it! And Practice DOES make Perfect!

My specialty as a dancer/stripper, was twerking. Click following link to watch me twerk in Magic City's dancer's dressing room! https://www.instagram.com/p/B41C2jQgk7I/
I remember when I was earning my Bachelor's in Entertainment Business online, many times I would take a break from a lesson, only to take that time and practice in the mirror. Many times, I'd be in that mirror, easily 2 or 3 hours learning how to "pop my

booty cheeks". I wanted to give the best performance possible, either on the floor or on stage. I wanted to give as many variations to twerking as possible when dancing for a customer. I wanted them to feel entertained. I perfected my twerking abilities so much so that other customers would stand off to the side staring in amazement and either wait their turn for me to come dance for them or tip me while I was dancing for that current customer. That was my hustle.

Whether it be twerking or pole work, the combination or whatever else, Practice it & Perfect it! Put time in, even outside of work, and watch it make a difference in your money! Become known for it. Learn your strengths, learn YOUR Hustle. I took my talents to Instagram and now here we are! As I type, 775K followers later. I know girls that have been featured in major celebrities' videos, tours, and some with roles/appearances on shows like, "P-Valley". You never know where these perfected talents, alone, can take you.

*** Check out my site www.twerkology101.com where I teach different variations of Twerking! ***

PRINCIPLE 2:

Walk that Walk! Be Assertive!

Hold your head up HIGH, Shoulders BACK, Chest OUT (don't overdo it), and walk one foot in front of the other. Your walk speaks volumes about how you feel about yourself, how confident or insecure you are. A confident walk is sexy and powerful as hell. When you walk into a room, you want your presence to be felt. When you get on that stage, you want to OWN IT! I had this special bounce-walk that I used to do on stage to get from one point to another quickly, but it was still sexy and entertaining. So much so the girls would emulate it and jokingly tease me about it.

Some will be intimidated by your assertiveness, others will adore it, but either way, many will remember you and your walk!

PRINCIPLE 3:

Master Stage Presence

I've seen so many girls get on that stage and TAKE OVER! ALL EYES ON THEM, mine included! There are two girls that come to mind; they had their own special walk and sensual movements that commanded attention, they would make eye contact with each and every one of their audiences who were captivated throughout their performance not daring for a second to take their eyes off them. They would smile seductively and mind-fuck their audience as they swayed and rotated their hips to the music causing their audience to, almost seemingly, blindly endlessly tip dollar after dollar, (or $5, $10, $20, whatever, you get the point.) It went down! Many times, thunderstorm and all!

One thing that these girls had in common and something that I admired most, was their confidence. They were in tune with their sensuality and sexuality…they OWNED IT and people responded, showing their appreciation with an overflow of dollar bills.

PRINCIPLE 4:

Appearance is EVERYTHING!!!

YOU are your product! How you present yourself to your audience matters! In the entertainment industry, you want to look your absolute best when it's showtime! You are a fantasy and must be "put together" at all times. I used to wear different dance outfits every time I worked, with different dance shoes to match. You gotta switch it up; people notice. Well, you don't HAVE to, but you will stand out from the competition. I got to the point where I had ladies making multiple outfits for me at least once a week. If you're just beginning, obviously, it takes time to build up this special wardrobe. (Tip: If you get tired of these outfits, you can always sell them later to other dancers, or you can now sell worn items online! $$$) How you treat yourself inwards reflects your outward appearance. Below are (some, obvious), tips to keep in mind on how to maintain an alluring appearance.

- Exercise / Stretch / Get Massages Often / Yoga / Nature / Meditate / Pray
- Drink Plenty of Water
- Do your hair!

    I didn't always get my hair done; my thing was a long, neat ponytail or classy side bun. This became part of my image, my signature look. I would do different things, I got creative; like adding a braid or a twist, some sparkly barrettes, along with the long ponytail down my back.

- Make sure you smell good, all of YOU.

    Good hygiene is an ABSOLUTE MUST! You don't have to wear expensive perfume or be sprayed down with body spray, but make sure you do not stink in any shape or form. Brush your teeth before you get to work or before you get on that floor. I always took a shower at home, brushed my teeth and all that before I got to work so that I was fresh and ready to go! A customer can get real turned off if ANY part of you smells bad. And you can most certainly build a bad reputation from smelling bad, alone. We don't want that!

- Exfoliate

    Even though I didn't really like being touched, it comes with the job, people just can't resist! I made sure my skin was always, smooth, soft and silky. When people did touch me, they'd be surprised. lol Dancers take care of themselves too! lol

- Eat a healthy diet

    I, personally, don't eat pork and beef. I love fruits, salads, avocados, vegetables. I don't eat fast food often, I do like my nuggets with that BBQ sauce from Chic-a-fila with that sweet lemonade, though! lol

- Take your vitamins
- Take Breaks often/Don't Burn Out

    When I first came to Atlanta, there was SO much money to get that I wasn't used to getting, I would work seven days a week! My schedule mainly consisted of sleeping and dancing. It was cool for a while, but I knew at some point, I needed to focus on my Exit Plan. (see Principle 21) I also knew I had to bring balance into my life. I weened myself off this schedule and reduced my days, throughout the years, down to 3. I gave my body a break. I would take time to educate myself and focus on things that would also bring me success. I would treat myself to vacations at least twice a year. I refreshed my energy from the club and every time I came back to work even after a couple days break, I felt refreshed and ready to tackle the night!

- Keep your Nails and Toes Done!

People notice, trust me! Guys LOVE a put together woman! Period.

- Clean, Neat Appearance

Always, Always, Always!!! Check your "Versace Wallet", as my girl Barbie used to call it (vagina, for those who are a little lost) before going on the floor! Check your teeth, your breath, check for stains of any kind, make sure tampon strings are tucked and hidden out of site! Change if you need to, or just because. Always wear clean, fresh dance outfits. Check all these things or have a friend check for you. Check your hair to make sure it's still in place, freshen lipstick or lip gloss…as many times as you need to, but not so much you miss out on money. Don't forget a mint or something like peppermint gum!

Click links below for videos of me in the Magic City dancer's dressing room!

https://www.instagram.com/p/CTVnkB6gGLg/
https://www.instagram.com/p/CVVpKYGgyog/

- Fresh, current & trendy work outfits

    Sustainability; maintain but also change with the times. You can have a signature look or signature outfits, but make sure you are also aware of and wear the styles of the current times. Make sure you have the right kind of stripper heels too! You don't want to look outdated, country or that you don't know what's going on. lol

- Mentality; positive self-talk

    Speak to yourself as you would to a beloved friend. Don't be obnoxious and self-centered but do love yourself and remain humble. How you feel about yourself inside is reflected on your outside appearance. You see yourself as an assertive, Money-Getting' Boss, so will they. (if they don't, doesn't matter, not your business) But, YOU set the tone! If they feel like they can take advantage, they will. Some will try you just for gp. (*general purpose) Positive self-talk helps keeps you strong and prepared.

- Self-educate; be a sponge, a constant learner of things!

    You will come across many people from different walks of life, so it doesn't hurt to know/learn a little something about everything. This is called investing in your human capital. The higher value of your human capital, the harder to replace. (this also ties into Principle 21 for the future) Of course, don't be a know it all, but have a little bit of intelligent conversation to offer. Don't forget to be a good listener too! This can add to the entertainment package as well. Use your discretion. (Be mindful of the time taken to have certain conversations; time is money now!) Never stay anywhere too long, unless you are getting paid!

PRINCIPLE 5:

Attitude is EVERYTHING!

One thing that I found while dancing in my 21 years, is that Attitude is EVERYTHING! I remember if I started the night off in a bad mood, that set the tone for the entire night. Leave whatever arguments or things that didn't go your way that day at the DOOR! Customers definitely notice. A bad attitude acts like a repellent to money; and we DON'T want that! We came to get that bread! People are drawn to both sexy, flirtatious smiles and warm, friendly hugs, not a mean mug. Use to your discretion with the hugs. I was and still am a hugger.

PRINCIPLE 6:

Teamwork Makes the Dream Work!

I'll say it again! Teamwork Makes the Dream Work! I used to love when all the girls would work together to make something happen and get ish done! No matter the number, 2, 5, 8, 10, 12, whatever! You dance together, you clean up together, and you straighten together! (this depends on the club) You help each other and you all can get to the next opportunity of money faster. Common curtesy goes a long way and people remember that. I remember many times, my thing was, if I had a pile and I was wrapping up to leave, there'd be a girl next to me with her own pile, I'd get a dollar or two from her, have her watch my pile and run to get a bag for both her and I. (use your discretion with who you do this with) Many times, the favor was returned.

Put somebody else on! After many years in the game, you get to know what types of girls certain customers liked. Many times, I'd say to a girl, "Hey, girl! I don't know, but you might want to go over there and introduce yourself. You are definitely their type! I can't make any guarantees, but you might just get picked to dance." Or if guys/customers would ask me if there were any new, bad females, I would point them out or go and get them. If I wasn't chosen to dance, I didn't care. I never minded putting someone else on. Feels good when you are able to help someone out and not to mention, karma notices too.

PRINCIPLE 7:

Secure Your Bag & your things! Literally!

You do not want to make it a habit just to leave your things out and unattended, unless you have no choice. Even though, we love our neighbor, you can't always trust them. People do steal. The best resolution to buy a lock and lock all your things up in a locker. You can also tip the house mom to watch your things, if the club has one and you trust her. I also used to secure my money on a garter wrapped around my ankle, secured by a rubber band. You could put it around your thigh, but the problem with that is people can walk by and take your money without you noticing if it becomes unsecure. Some girls carry money bags around with them, but, if you set it down and forget it, it will most likely disappear. Whatever your preference, Secure your money!

PRINCIPLE 8:

Promote Your Brand; Social Media, word-of-mouth

One way to make more money in the club, is to use social media. We didn't always have social media, but we still had other ways of getting our names out there. Back in the day, though, I would run from the camera. lol Putting myself out there was, 1) not widely accepted, and 2) not part of what I wanted to the world to know about me. After one of those bad nights at the club and still trying to figure out my exit plan, I went home to meditate and came across an online certification program where I learned about Strategic Social Media Marketing. Once I knew how I could leverage my dancing, I put my inhibitions to the side and made ish happen. With regards to my main goal, I used myself as a test subject. I had to OWN who I was and put my strategy into place.

I married my dancer name to the infamous club I worked at and now people from far and wide ask about me at that very same club today. Social media is a powerful tool, learn it, understand it, and use it to your advantage…for whatever your reason. I guarantee, if you do it right, your opportunities and money will multiply. Below are the following links to my different social media platforms. Click any or all of the links below, Follow & Subscribe!

Sexy Red 🍷 (@sexyred_magiccity1) • Instagram photos and videos

Sexy Red Magic Cit (@sexyred_magiccity) TikTok | Watch Sexy Red Magic Cit's Newest TikTok Videos

Sexy Red Magic City - YouTube

Sexy Red (@SexyRed_mc) / Twitter

SexyRed OnlyFans

https://www.facebook.com/sexyredbackup

PRINCIPLE 9:

Use the club to Network

So many people from all walks of life go to the strip club. Your friends, their friends, street dudes, businessmen and women, lawyers, doctors, teachers, college students, jays, you name it. The rich and famous always stop through, whether it be actors, comedians, athletes, rappers, singers, producers...you name it! I was awarded many opportunities by dancing in the club; I worked as a production assistant on BET's Sunday Best for a few shows, appeared in a documentary that has aired in the UK a few times about dancers at the club I worked at, I appeared in a reality show but decided it wasn't for me once they wanted to "up" the ratings by causing a bit of chaos, but an opportunity most wouldn't pass up. As I mentioned in Principle 1, I know girls that were featured in popular rappers' videos, went on tour to perform on the pole for some famous artists, about 3 that appeared in "P-Valley", some girls had cleaning services that they would solicit to gain that type of clientele, and that's just to name a few opportunities. You network and talk to the right people; one never knows what the future can hold.

PRINCIPLE 10:

Always, Always, Be Aware of your surroundings!

People forget, the strip club can be a very dangerous place to work. Be mindful of your surroundings. Do not drink to the point of intoxication. For one, you can miss out on money and, for two, people are not always watching you for entertainment purposes. Whether you drink or not, be mindful of what and who you do it with AND your surroundings! Dancers can make a lot of money the average Joe may not be aware of. Some people know what kind of money dancers make and will prey on them. Some men and women prey on women for other reasons, unfortunately, that is the nature of the beast. Keep mace, a hammer, a bat, scissors, whatever you feel comfortable with in hidden places in your car to ward off someone trying to harm you. Have a security guard walk you to your car and tip them generously. You must always be aware; anything can and will happen. Don't allow a lot of people to know where you live and if you can, don't always take the same route home. If you can, text, call or drop your location (if you stop/go somewhere other than home) with a friend or family member until you make it home safe and sound.

PRINCIPLE 11:

Don't take everything to heart, or personal.

Just because you do not get picked to dance in a group or you don't get to dance for your favorite celebrity, don't take it personal. Shrug it off and keep it pushing. You never know, you could luck up on a major pile all to yourself! It does happen. And you never know, (yes, we all go to work to make money), but sometimes, others may need it more than you.

Sometimes, customers have preferences. Don't take it to heart. It's their money, they are entitled to spend it how they wish. Everybody ain't for everybody, but YOU are for sure somebody's type! What is meant for you will never pass you by. Remember that! If someone wants to give you money, they will make sure you get it. Period, point blank.

PRINCIPLE 12:

Don't bring a gun to a knife fight; choose your battles!

Remember! You came to the club to make money, not to beat females' asses! It's not worth it to get suspended or fired because you had to put hands on somebody. Fighting is not worth the time, the energy, or the loss of money. It can even sometimes land you in a courtroom. Ain't nobody got time for that! It's not cute in any shape or form. Now, to defend yourself, that's another story. Sometimes you gotta be the bigger person in a situation, and take a monetary loss in an argument, but it's better to take that over bumps, bruises, court fees, and missed workdays. It doesn't matter if a disagreement is over your man, her man, her "customer", your money, somebody's said somebody's child is ugly…Doesn't Matter! In all my 21 years of dancing, I've not gotten into one single fight. You have to learn to control yourself and your emotions. It's never that serious, trust me.

PRINCIPLE 13:

Do things you like; things that make YOU feel good.

One thing I did that many dancers may disagree with is, perfume. Many dancers don't wear perfume or sprays because they don't want to get it on the customer. Not me. lol I would spray on my most favorite perfume when I worked. Many times, they were quite expensive, but I didn't care. Why only save the good stuff for special occasions? Smelling my best, made me feel my best. I also, would damn near, douse myself in baby oil. I loved the way my skin felt and glistened. It made my skin soft, supple and irresistible. I liked glitter too. teehehe Not for nothing, my perfume, glitter and baby oil caused a lot of people NOT to touch me. That, I liked very much so. You can't do this in all clubs, but the ones I worked at, I did.

PRINCIPLE 14:

Cater to your customers; pay special attention to them AND their lady guests.

People LOVE when you remember their name, most people anyway. Greet the club's customers with a smile and be genuinely charming. Whether you know the guests' name or not, be hospitable and accommodating. If they need drinks, a waitress, money, a seat, do what it takes to make them feel comfortable so they can comfortably have a good time. Another tip, is if a male customer has female guests with him, DO NOT ignore them! Be just as nice to them as your gentlemen guest. They came to have a good time too!

PRINCIPLE 15:

Exclusivity: Don't allow yourself to be SMUTTED out

You are a fantasy and a lot of men, sometimes women, may want to make that fantasy a reality! Use your own judgement and intuition; ultimately, exclusivity is KING. Some men like to be met with a challenge; the game to possess what no one else can or have what no one else has had. They are turned on so much so they will give you money, and more money, and even more money after that to get that prize! And yes, relationships do come about in the club, but it's best to keep that limited. And if you do get into a relationship, it's probably best to keep it to yourself because if it gets out, it WILL affect your money…negatively. At least, in my case, it did. And if you're single, STILL remain exclusive, YES, you will lose out on money/"opportunities", but better that than to kill your reputation and burn out. (*this is just my advice, but that is your vagina, not mine. Obviously, do as you wish with it.) You can most certainly make a lot of money with the "effing all the ninjas with a lot of money" method, and deal with the rest later…not recommended but again, that's your business. A lot of new girls are faced with this issue, especially ones that are pretty with super nice bodies. Get to know who's who before making ANY moves. Become familiarized with who the big tippers are, the regulars, who's homies with who, and who the "time wasters" are. And then make a move, should you choose to do so. And if not, it's still beneficial to know who's who.

PRINCIPLE 16:

Body Enhancements; Do what makes YOU happy.

Body enhancements do make a difference for some in this industry and can be a great investment in yourself. Some girls shared with me that their money was the same after surgery. I guess it all depends. Maybe some exude more confidence, some actually do look that much better. My suggestion is really just to do your homework on it. Be mindful, some nasty scarring may occur, or lumps and dents may appear and ask yourself are these some of the side effects you're willing to accept. Some things, you can't go back after you've made whatever enhancement. Some surgeries look perfect. So, make sure either way, it's not just to see an increase in your money or because you think someone else would think you're sexier with enhancements but also, you want to get surgery or body enhancements because YOU want it/them.

PRINCIPLE 17:

Do NOT make promises you cannot keep!

I highly recommend NOT to make promises you do not intend on keeping! For one, it is very dangerous, especially, with people you do not know. Girls will tell guys/customers all the time that they'll go home with them just so the customer can keep giving them money. I've even seen "Baby Strippers" laugh and brag about it on TikTok. All I could do was shake my head. Customers will literally wait outside for you. There was one true story where this happened, and the girl was killed. Everybody don't play and just say they're going to charge it to the game. Sis, take that lil "L", don't do it, get your bread from the next customer or come back another night. It's not that serious…unless that's the type of thing you're into. No judgement here, but keep in mind, your safety is first!

PRINCIPLE 18:

Know your Worth!

One thing people forget about the strip club, is that you don't have to dance for any and everybody in the club. If that's your hustle, then kudos to you. But this is something you don't HAVE to do. I always felt like I was the one choosing who I wanted to entertain. And just because you are dancing for someone, you have to allow them to do any and everything to you because they "paid" for it. You still deserve respect and deserve to be treated as such. Just because you are a dancer does not mean you are to be treated with any form of disrespect.

Your body is a temple; for dancers or adult entertainers, we allow people to view the most precious parts of ourselves. People, both men and women, praise and give thanks (in the form of money) to our wonderful, sensual, majestic temples. You have to WANT to entertain; it has to come from deep within just like with anything else, or else it transfers over into something that seems to be forced and you surely won't last long. Take pride in your temple, KNOW YOUR WORTH, and others will follow suit.

If you weren't aware, dancing can actually be a form of helping someone heal. Who would've thunk?! But its true! We help people take their minds off things. We contribute to saving marriages by helping women become more in touch with their sexuality. We teach them how to dance and entertain their husbands bringing back a little spice in their sex AND love life. Sometimes, simply by us offering a listening ear can be helpful therapy for some. Never look down at yourself for being a dancer. There is healing that can be found in the art of adult entertainment.

PRINCIPLE 19:

Don't become a lush!

Granted you're in a club environment, there is liquor (and drugs all around), but that doesn't mean you have to overdo it or even partake in consumption. You don't HAVE to do anything you do not want to do. Sometimes groups may want you to drink shots to stay in the group. Use your discretion. If you walk away, yeah, you may lose out on money from that section. But guess what?! If you don't get it there, you can always get it somewhere else! And if not that same night, if you keep coming back, you WILL get your night!

Some girls feel like they "need" a drink or something to start their night off…BIG NO NO! This can lead to a life of addiction, and everything is downhill from that point. People can/will take advantage of you, they will steal from you, you're not able to drive home (can lead to DUIs fines and other restrictions), you can hurt yourself and/or others, people can hurt you, etc.…you get my point. I remember one time, this girl was so intoxicated, she fell down the steps and busted her chin. If I'm not mistaken, she broke 2 front teeth as well. When in the club, you gotta know your limit; it's just not worth it. Sadly, some people are just trying to mask the pain of their personal story. This type of behavior only making it worse. I was the type, if no one offered me a drink, I just didn't have alcohol that night. Many times, I would detox from alcohol and politely say no when a drink was offered. Not for nothing, hella people respected my decision. Gotta keep your mind sharp and on point in this world. The point is, you can have fun and enjoy yourself, but you are there to get your money and get home safely so you can go back and do it all again the next time. P.S. Your liver and your future face will thank you later!

And let us NOT forget to add this tip while we're on the subject! NEVER turn your back on your drink, should you choose to drink! Anybody can, very quickly and discretely, slip something in there that can have you running down the street naked or worse! Once you turn your back or take your eyes off your drink...you're done. Throw it in the garage and order another one.

PRINCIPLE 20:

Sometimes You Gotta Take the Good with the Bad.

Every night is not going to be a "good" night. Keep in mind, a good night is dependent upon the individual. To some $1,000 is a good night, to others $3,000, and so on and so forth; it all depends. Regardless of your definition of a "good" night, you WILL have bad nights. Sometimes, you may even end the night owing money. It is what it is, don't take it to heart, just come back again another day. It also doesn't hurt to start focusing on a backup plan in your spare time, which is was a habit I kept.

Everything happens for a reason, even the bad nights. I remember one night; I had SUCH a bad night! I was normally pretty good at handling those types of nights, but this one hit different. I went home early to mediate and came across an online certification program about Strategic Social Media Marketing…changed my life forever! Two years later, after only completing 25% of the program, give or take a few details, in just one year I made over a half a million dollars online! That's quite a bag! (side tip: everyone doesn't need to know exactly what your pockets are looking like, but for the sake of making a point, I needed to share that with you) Once you understand the ebbs and flows of the business, everything becomes a lot easier. Don't wallow in self-pity, thinking about all the reasons why you didn't make good money that night, do something positive with that time. Turn lemons into lemonade! Find and take opportunities where you can, you never know what the future may have in store for you.

PRINCIPLE 21:

Have an Exit Plan.

No matter how long it takes, take advantage of the flexible schedule dancing offers and have or create an exit plan. When I first started dancing in Atlanta, I would work seven (7) days a week; 5 at then, Body Tap, and 2 at Strokers. I was on my SUPER HUSTLE! At some point, I knew I needed to take advantage of this schedule. I decided to narrow down my days to 4, then 3. I discovered what I wanted to focus on outside of dancing. I ended up successfully completing a 4-year degree in 2 and a half, with Academic Honors.

Additionally, dancing can most certainly turn into a career but just like an athlete, year after year can incur a great deal of wear and tear. Dancing, and even worse, pole dancing, can take a toll on the body. You must look deep inside yourself, again, discover what you're good at outside of dancing or like me, along side the dancing model, and create an exit plan. This e-book you're reading is an example of an exit plan. I'm not physically dancing in a club anymore, but nonetheless, dancing created this opportunity. The world is FULL of opportunities, you just have to recognize them, hone in on the right ones for you and EXECUTE. Invest in educating yourself, whether it be through a conventional institution or self-education (i.e. certifications, online programs offered by reputable gurus, YouTube how-to videos, etc.), and NEVER STOP learning. Be patient with yourself and the process, as many of these opportunities take time to build, that is why it is important to start building your solid foundation while you have that extra free time your dancing schedule offers.

BONUS PRINCIPLE:

Visualize and Materialize.

My Bonus Principle and final tip. Something I used to do when I was on my way to work, was imagine a bunch of ones falling on my back. I allowed myself to be in the energy of making LOTS of money…literally see myself swimming in it. Every night I worked I would visualize this and me gathering and counting pile after pile of money at the end of the night. I can't count how many times this was my reality. I still do this with other goals in my life and watch as my dreams literally turn into my reality. It worked for me and if you believe, it too can work for you! Happy, Safe Stripping!

ABOUT THE AUTHOR

So! You've decided you want to be a stripper and you're just getting started but you'd like a few pointers before you get to the bag. You want credible information from a reliable source. Well, my friend you've come to the right place! I go by the name of Sexy Red Magic City, and I have danced in the hottest clubs in the game for 21 years! I have a Bachelor's in Entertainment Business, have a bit of knowledge in Strategic Social Media Marketing which, among other things, has allowed me to build an impressive following on Instagram, TikTok, Twitter, and Onlyfans. I have a thriving Shopify and Amazon store https://shop.thesexyredbrand.com , I am known by the masses, both online and offline, mainly for my twerking skills which I will be offering online tutorials where one can learn different variations of twerking. I also have created my own NFTs as well as have my own collection of NFTs purchased from other creators. So, look no further! In this book, I break down all the things you should be aware of and things you should know in order to lead a healthy, successful career as a stripper no matter how long you choose to dance! Welcome to the world of stripping, New Booties on Duty!

www.ingramcontent.com/pod-product-compliance
Lightning Source LLC
Chambersburg PA
CBHW042324150426
43192CB00001B/41